INDIAN CITY USA

INDIAN CITY USA

DR. BOBBIE CHEW BIGBY AND RANDY PALMER

ARCADIA
PUBLISHING

Published by Arcadia Publishing
Charleston, South Carolina

Printed in the United States of America

Library of Congress Control Number: 2024936957

For all general information, please contact Arcadia Publishing:
Telephone 843-853-2070
Fax 843-853-0044
E-mail sales@arcadiapublishing.com

Visit us on the Internet at www.arcadiapublishing.com

*To all those who worked out at Indian City and made
it the special place it was and continues to be*

CONTENTS

ACKNOWLEDGMENTS

This book is built upon the memories, experiences, and stories of those who called Indian City home. Sincere thanks go to the entire Palmer family and particularly to Glenda, Katherine, Carla, and Dixon Owen as well as Stephanie Tahbone. Gratitude also to Pamela Chew for her continuous support from the dissertation writing to postcard collection phases and beyond. A big thank-you to Lester Harragarra for allowing us to feature some of his beautiful photographs of the Kiowa Black Leggings Warrior Society. The co-authors are deeply grateful to the Kiowa Tribe and the Kiowa Black Leggings Warrior Society for their support of this project. In particular, we are thankful to several key collaborators in this project who were part of the Indian City family and who generously shared their time and memories with us. This includes Dorothy Whitehorse Delaune, Bruce and Arlene "Susie" Caesar, Donna Jean Tsatoke, and Lois Tsatoke. Tim Nestell's enthusiasm, stories, and assistance with documenting parts of the project have been particularly appreciated. Blas Preciado and Kent Sanmann are also appreciated for their assistance and early conversations that helped to lead the project to its next steps.

This project would not have been possible without the unwavering support of Dr. Bryan Grimwood and the Department of Recreation and Leisure Studies at the University of Waterloo, who walk the talk when it comes to encouraging and enabling community-based research and scholarship. This work has been supported by a Social Sciences and Humanities Research Council of Canada Insight Grant (435-2018-0616) entitled "Unsettling Tourism: Settler Stories, Indigenous Lands, and Awakening an Ethics of Reconciliation."

This project began with Bobbie's PhD dissertation journey, which focused on Indigenous tourism both in Oklahoma and Australia. Conversations, interviews, and meals with the Palmer family led to a shared ambition to be able to document and share the memories of Indian City with wider audiences and, in particular, the Native American youth of Anadarko and surrounding areas. In putting this book together, Randy serves as the primary storyteller, sharing his memories and images, while Bobbie serves as the writer, researcher, interviewer, and organizer. As co-authors, we acknowledge that we were unable to identify every single name and tribal affiliation(s) of each person pictured in the images, even though efforts and consultations were made. Any oversights in the text are the sole responsibility of the co-authors. Unless noted, all images appear courtesy of Randy Palmer.

INTRODUCTION

If you ask almost anyone who worked at Indian City USA over its nearly 55-year history what they remember of the place, their responses quickly become emotional, sentimental, and filled with deep memories.

"I grew up at Indian City, I learned so much there. It was such a wonderful, special place," Tim Nestell said.

"Indian City was my second home. That was my family, all those people out there. There's all kinds of history around here," according to Randy Palmer.

The Native American cultural attraction of Indian City USA sits on a landscape that is layered with the histories and cultural ties of numerous tribes. The name of "Indian City USA" itself owes its existence to the fact that it is located on the outskirts of Anadarko, a town in southwestern Oklahoma often dubbed the "Indian Capital of the Nation." Anadarko is officially home to the tribal government headquarters of the Wichita and Affiliated Tribes, the Apache Tribe of Oklahoma (often referred to as the Plains or Kiowa Apache), and the Delaware Nation. However, in and around the Anadarko area of southwestern Oklahoma can also be found the Kiowa, Caddo, Chiricahua (Fort Sill) Apache, and Comanche Nations, among other tribes who have intermarried or share cultural connections.

Long before the start of this Native American cultural attraction, however, the area near where Indian City sits was the site of the Tonkawa Massacre of 1862. The homelands of the Tonkawa Tribe were originally in Texas, but the community had been forcibly relocated to Indian Territory (now Oklahoma) in 1859. Settled along the Washita River near Fort Cobb, the Tonkawas found few allies among the other southern plains tribes. Apart from the fear that the Tonkawas instilled in other tribes, they were also disliked by neighboring tribes for having sided with the Confederacy during the US Civil War that was playing out. Senior Kiowa elder Dorothy Whitehorse Delaune recounted that in 1862, word spread that the Tonkawa Tribe had kidnapped a young Caddo boy. Enraged by this, the Caddos called for help from other tribes, and a group of Delaware, Comanche, Shawnee, and other tribal members united to help free the boy and fight the Tonkawas. This force attacked and overwhelmed the Tonkawa people, killing an estimated half of the population of approximately 367. The weakened remaining Tonkawa community was finally resettled in its current reservation jurisdiction in north-central Oklahoma in 1884 and is one of the 38 different federally recognized tribes in Oklahoma today. This is why to this day, the creek that runs through the Indian City area is named Tonkawa Creek.

The idea for what was to become Indian City originated with several Anadarko businessmen. Often referred to as Anadarko's "city fathers," these city leaders envisioned a place that would serve two purposes—an initiative that would allow Native people of the area to preserve cultural traditions while providing the opportunity for non-Native people to come, learn, and interact with tribal cultures. Even though the majority of the Indian City board was comprised of non-Native people for much of its run, Kiowa elder Delaune maintained that the relationships, camaraderie, and mutual respect between the Native people and the non-Native management were extremely strong. An important example of these positive relationships included the memories many recounted with George Moran and his family, including his son George "Sonny" Moran Jr. They managed and ran the enterprise over decades and were well-loved fixtures of Indian City. Thus, from its beginning, Indian City was an extremely unique venture that was based largely on the collaboration of Anadarko residents—Native and non-Native—working together toward shared goals that sat within a tourism business structure.

Indian City USA opened on July 2, 1955, and sat within a 160-acre tract of land. From early on, Indian City was deeply intertwined with the business and cultural life of Anadarko. Strong cooperation was maintained not just between Indian City employees and its board of directors but also with the Anadarko city leaders and chamber of commerce, as well as with the other cultural sites in town. These other cultural attractions included the Southern Plains Indian Museum, the Indian Hall of Fame, and the annual American Indian Exposition—places and events that have held both cultural significance for locals and tourism appeal for visitors into the present.

Some of the first people to work at Indian City included the Buffalo family, in particular Delores Buffalo, the most recognized tour guide and one of Indian City's well-loved faces. A member of the Otoe-Missouria Tribe, Delores was known for her talents not only as a tour guide but also as a seamstress, hide tanner, bead worker, feather worker, and tipi maker. She had learned how to make tipis from her Kiowa mother-in-law, Mary Buffalo, and worked alongside her husband, Homer, over the years. Many of these cultural skills were also taught and passed on to her children. When asked about working at Indian City, Delores was quoted in *Oklahoma Today* in 1980 as saying, "I've had lots of other [job] offers, but they're inside. I like this because it's outside and I meet nice people and in the winter when there's not too many [tourists] coming, I have time to do crafts. Besides I don't get bored because there's always something different every day." Delores's words point to one of the most important aspects of daily life at Indian City: it enabled and supported a flourishing of Native-made arts, crafts, foods, and other cultural traditions.

Renowned Pawnee silversmith and jeweler Bruce Caesar recounted that his family had their own shop selling jewelry at Indian City for many years. Descending from a family of notable metalsmiths and recognized as a National Heritage Fellow by the National Endowment for the Arts, Bruce's career in metalsmithing and jewelry spans nearly six decades and got its start at Indian City. According to Bruce, his late father, noted Pawnee silversmith Julius Caesar, had moved his entire family to Anadarko to come to work at Indian City. There on the premises, he taught his sons metalsmithing and they sold their hand-made jewelry to the large numbers of visitors that came and toured daily. Bruce shared, "Just being a seven-year-old kid, working for my dad and learning from him, alongside my brother, learning the techniques of traditional jewelry-making . . . that was the fun part of being able to control your own destiny in that you didn't have to work in the grocery store or out in the fields . . . you could sit there and create stuff. . . . Indian City helped people like us who were artists to have a niche, a place to make our livelihood through the summer tourism months, and even through the winter months."

For Bruce, this family jewelry business not only brought his family financial stability and success but also enabled him to hone his own skills and craftsmanship from a young age. It also allowed him to grow up connected with the dancers, singers, and other cultural practitioners of Anadarko who similarly made their livelihood at Indian City. Wife Arlene "Susie" Caesar's family ran the concession stand alongside her mother, Agatha Bates. Together, they made and sold food to thousands of hungry customers, including fry bread, hot dogs, and hamburgers that were known as the most delicious in town.

Tribal arts and crafts were not only on display at the museum and gift shop within the Indian City Lodge, as well as among independent vendors such as the Caesars, but also thrived through the Indian City Pottery enterprise. Begun in 1971 after Indian City management struggled to obtain enough pottery stock to meet the high sales demand in its gift shop, Indian City initiated the pottery plant as a multi-agency effort with support provided by the Bureau of Indian Affairs, US Department of the Interior, and the Oklahoma State Vocational Education Division. Student employees were trained in all aspects of wheel-thrown pottery making and painting, with no molds ever used. Pottery was decorated with elaborate designs, painted figures, and tribal stories. Pieces regularly for sale and in demand included not only pots and vases of various sizes but also ashtrays, wall plaques, and special commissions.

The Palmer family was one of the most active families across all aspects of the Indian City experience, from the dancing, tipi painting, and regalia making to the management and mentorship of young, up-and-coming dancers. Randy Palmer, a Kiowa veteran and culture keeper, reflected on how his late father, Dixon Palmer, taught him to dance from the time he was just learning to walk. From 1955 to 1973, Dixon worked as head guide at Indian City before later becoming assistant manager, a duty that he shared with his wife, Chlotiea, as co-assistant manager. Apart from their management leadership, the Palmer family dancers—including Dixon and his brother George, along with all of their children—were considered to be one of the star attractions for any visitor coming to Indian City. Known for their quick, skillful movements and brightly colored regalia, the Palmer family dancers were a fixture of Indian City performances but also traveled the United States showing audiences southern plains Native American dances.

Beyond just learning about his own Kiowa heritage and cultural traditions, Randy also grew up immersed in and appreciating the diverse tribal traditions that were shared among the different families in Indian City. One of the most important examples of this ongoing intertribal learning was that he and many of the other young people learned how to build each other's traditional tribal dwellings, such as the Wichita grass house and Apache wikiup. This intertribal sharing of knowledge, traditions, languages, and arts was part of daily life at Indian City. It is what made it such a unique gathering place and a center of both employment and learning for many in the community. According to Kiowa elder Delaune, the makeup of Indian City as an intertribal destination, bringing together the different tribes of the area and their diverse cultural knowledge, was an essential part of what gave Indian City its strength over decades.

Indian City was deeply important to so many in the Anadarko Native American community because it was seen by many locals as a site of cultural perpetuation, community-building, and resurgence. "Resurgence" is a term that Cherokee Nation scholar Jeff Corntassel explains as connections and reconnections to community, traditional culture, and land-based lifeways among Indigenous peoples. Fundamentally, Indian City's strength in providing a base for cultural perpetuation was enabled through its model as a tourism enterprise. Functioning as a tourism enterprise that generated revenues from visitors wanting to see and learn about Native culture, this cultural tourism model was able to provide local livelihoods to community members. Anadarko Native people who worked at Indian City could support their families based on the income earned from sharing and staying connected to traditional Native culture—something that was and can still be challenging to find in other mainstream employment options available, whether in rural or urban Oklahoma. Sharing dances, pottery, traditional songs, and stories with tourists literally allowed local people to put food on their own tables at home. As pointed out by Bruce Caesar, this legacy of cultural resurgence linked to tourism and other economic initiatives was kick-started by Indian City but has continued into the present through the cultural tourism initiatives of other tribes and intertribal alliances throughout Oklahoma.

This linking of cultural resurgence and economic empowerment together also resulted in another aspect of the Indian City legacy shared by so many: a deep sense of pride. Pride is reflected very clearly in the words of lead guide Delores Buffalo, who was quoted in a 1980 *Oklahoma Today* article as saying, "As an Indian, you're proud of what you are. That's why I like it here. Indian City is the history of the American Indian!" Kiowa elder Delaune countered the perception sometimes articulated in the public that those Native people who worked at Indian City were treated and viewed only as Native American performers playing to the stereotypes of Native culture in the American media. Delaune emphatically stated, "Some people said that [Indian City] exploited us. That isn't true!" One of the most vivid examples of this sense of pride in working at Indian City was illustrated through a memory shared by Lois Tsatoke. Tsatoke recounted that in 1973, activists from Native tribes outside of Oklahoma had come through Anadarko and tried to recruit local Native people to join their activities. These out-of-state activists tried to persuade some of the people working at Indian City that they should leave, claiming that Indian City looked like a place where Native people were being exploited and forced to play to the stereotypes Americans wanted to see. Tsatoke was one of the voices to push back on this claim, saying that from her perspective there was no exploitation going on and that she was proud to be working alongside family members in sharing her culture while earning a paycheck. According to Randy Palmer, some of the young performers on site had earned a paycheck since they were two years old.

But speaking to Indian City's importance for the Anadarko Native community only reflects one side of a two-sided coin. Equally as significant were Indian City's impacts on the countless tourists and visitors—non–Native Americans from across the country and globe—who came and learned about tribal cultures year after year, busload after busload. For many tourists, a trip to Indian City could represent their first and perhaps the only time in their lives to meet a Native American person and learn about Native culture outside of the common and inaccurate stereotypes presented in mainstream American media, education, and popular culture. Delores Buffalo was known to be "quick to put down any tourist who shows disrespect for Indian ways" but also equally quick to share insights and humor and be approachable to children and the elderly alike. Randy Palmer shared that so much of his work talking to visitors revolved around educating people that not all Native people lived in tipis. Through his work as a performer and tour guide, Randy helped to inform visitors about the diversity of tribal cultures and languages, not just at Indian City but across the United States.

In these daily processes of interactions and education through tourism over decades, it can be argued that countless visitors were likely impacted before Indian City closed its doors in the late 2000s. Referencing the reflections of Delores after nearly 35 years of guiding tourists, a 1980 article from *Oklahoma Today* magazine wrote, "Mrs. Buffalo has noticed a change in non-Indian attitudes lately. More and more, they reveal a positive outlook where Indians are concerned. Many come looking not just for souvenirs, but for ideas they can use to survive in the modern world." Indian City thus played a part in helping to open the eyes of visitors who might be curious, eager to learn, ill-informed, or totally unaware of the rich diversity of Native American cultures. Moreover, the interactive experiences and engagements afforded to visitors by tourism offered opportunities for learning and shifting perceptions—helping to put a spotlight on the brilliance contained within tribal knowledge and lifeways as well as the resilience of the communities who still carry these important ways forward.

These processes of cultural resurgence and the perpetuation of Native arts, dances, languages, foodways, stories, values, and worldviews remain vital objectives for the younger Native generations not only of Anadarko but across Oklahoma and United States Indian Country. Informed by this legacy of cultural pride and economic empowerment fostered at Indian City, we as co-authors offer this book as a celebration of this important place. Indian City was significant not only because it became a center of culture and community for so many but also because it stands as a unique and truly rare example of an economic model that over several decades supported these connections to culture and community. Bobbie and Randy hope that these memories, images, and stories help to inspire the next generations to remain strong and connected to the beautiful living cultures of their Native communities.

One

Proud Faces of
Indian City USA

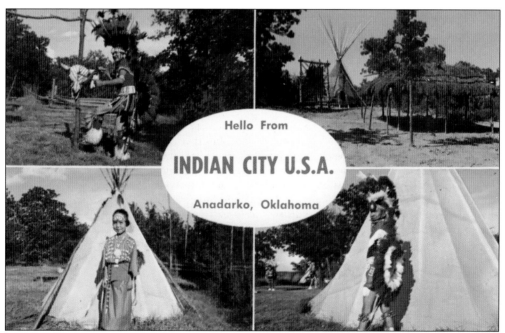

Indian City was made up of proud people and proud faces that had the opportunity to share the diversity of Native American cultures with the wider world. Over its nearly 55-year legacy, Indian City welcomed hundreds of thousands of tourists year-round, particularly during the peak summer months. Regardless of tribal affiliation or age, every person working at Indian City had the opportunity to share about their culture and community.

When visitors arrived to Indian City, they would follow a winding road before finally coming onto the second hill, where the Indian City Lodge and villages were located. Indian City's location atop this hill gave it a wonderful vantage point for visitors to look out across the Anadarko area.

Inside the Indian City Lodge was a museum and gift shop that sold a wide variety of Native-made arts and crafts, including the unique decorated pottery that was made on-site. The small museum contained a variety of southern plains Native American art and items used in all aspects of traditional life, including rare items such as horse bridles made of twisted horsehair.

Atop the roof of the Indian City Lodge was a thunderbird design. For numerous tribes in the area, the thunderbird is a symbol of power and good luck. In Oklahoma, the thunderbird is also commonly seen as the key symbol of the 45th Infantry Brigade Combat Team, which is part of the Oklahoma Army National Guard.

Kiowa dancer Paul Paddlety stands in front of the Indian City Lodge entrance, ready to greet visitors before they begin their 45-minute tour departing from the lodge. Each day during the peak summer season there were eight tours that would be led and four different dance performances.

Delores Buffalo was one of the best-known faces of Indian City and the most experienced guide, having been part of Indian City since its opening. Delores belonged to the Otoe-Missouria Tribe but married into a Kiowa family. She and her husband, Homer Buffalo, were known for making over 400 tipis by hand. She walked the half-mile tour trail every day, up to eight times a day with different tour groups during the summer and up to four times a day during the winter. Delores started as a guide in 1958 and served as a guide up until she was in her 90s.

The Palmer family stood at the heart of Indian City as dancers, performers, managers, pottery makers, and storytellers. Dixon Palmer (center) stands with his children, Randy (left) and Lynda (right), at the Kiowa village and speaks about the importance of the bison to Kiowa people and culture. He points to a stretched bison hide that was on display in the Kiowa winter camp area.

Several members of the Palmer family were known as excellent traditional dancers in addition to skilled regalia makers. Lynda Palmer (left) stands watching her uncle George and cousin Vincent (center) as her father, Dixon (right), provides the drumming. Nearly all pieces of the regalia worn by the family were handmade by the dancers themselves, ranging from featherwork and beadwork to sourcing the bells, leather, and other adornments.

Dixon shows his daughter, Lynda, a stretched bison hide on display in the Kiowa village. Before the forced removals and reservation era, several of the plains Native American tribes such as the Kiowa would follow the movements of the bison. Kiowas depended on this animal for all aspects of life, both material and spiritual, as the gifts offered by the bison could provide sustenance, shelter, and tools for life on the southern plains.

Young Vincent Palmer is dressed in full regalia and dances the steps of an eagle dance that he is learning from his father and uncle. His arms are adorned with eagle feathers and extended to show him mimicking the flight of an eagle as he dances.

Two young Native American girls proudly stand showing their regalia. To the left, the young girl's pink dress is adorned with cowrie shells across the chest. The regalia of many plains Native American women is often adorned on top with items that held traditional value and were hard to find, including elk teeth and cowrie shells. A belt was also worn by plains Native American girls and women, fastened with important small bags and items essential for everyday use. Below, the young dancer wears her shawl as is appropriate for ladies, young and old, when moving about the dance arena and dancing around the drum.

A woman and a young girl of the Kiowa Tribe walk together hand-in-hand in front of a tipi in the Kiowa camp. Both ladies wear beaded medallion necklaces, but the young girl wears a cloth traditional dress, while the woman's buckskin dress is adorned with several intricately beaded medallions. Both cloth and buckskin regalia alike were commonly worn at Indian City.

Bessie Keyonnie, a Navajo mother and weaver, looks after her young baby boy, Juan Diego Keyonnie, who is wrapped snugly in his cradleboard. Both are inside of a traditional Navajo hogan dwelling located in the Indian City village. Navajos have an extensive tradition of weaving elaborate patterns and creating textiles that are used as clothing and rugs.

Donna Jean Tsatoke is pictured with her daughters, Anna, Ladonna, and Lois, at the pond near the Caddo village, where she worked most of the time. Donna remembered that during the hot summer months, she and her children would often sit under the shade of the arbor in the Caddo village as tourists would come through.

Kiowa dancer Redwing Hahtogo demonstrates an eagle dance pose in front of a painted tipi in the Kiowa village.

Kiowa brothers Henry and J.O. Tanedoah were also known by the community as White Cloud (left) and Swimming Bear (right). They are pictured together in front of a tipi. Both men wear full war bonnets, denoting their standing in the tribal community.

Ernie Keahbone (left) and Dixon Palmer (right) stand in front of a tipi with Dixon carrying a spear and hand-painted shield. Both men wear breastplates that were traditionally made of bison bone. These breastplates functioned as a type of protective armor in combat, as they could help lessen the blows from hits by a tomahawk or deflect arrows.

Lee Tsatoke Jr. practices his war dance moves in front of a tipi painted by Dixon Palmer. Lee grew up to be a war dance champion and an accomplished artist. The Kiowa last name "Tsatoke" can also be written "Tsain toke e" and can be translated as "Hunting Horse." Lee's father and grandfather were also artists, with his grandfather Monroe Tsatoke representing one of the original famed Kiowa Five (also known as the Kiowa Six) artists.

Dixon Palmer stands in his full regalia ready to demonstrate a war dance. Dixon had a strong reputation not only for being a talented dancer and performer but also for his skills in creating his regalia. Many dancers made every piece of their regalia by hand and paid attention to the details so their regalia would reflect their family, stories, and identity.

Two young men adorned in their full dance regalia pose on the side of the hill at Indian City. Another designation commonly used to refer to Indian City as a "proving ground for champions" among powwow dancers. Indian City was known to be a place not only where young dancers could get their start but also where they could refine their dance moves before going on to perform across the country.

Lynda Palmer (left) looks on as her father, Dixon (center), drums while her brother, Randy (right), practices his dance moves and footwork. Several of the dances commonly seen and taught at Indian City, including the shield dance, are dances that are no longer often seen at powwows and cultural gatherings.

Young dancers, such as this little boy, learned to dance at Indian City from the time that they could walk. Children who accompanied their parents, siblings, and other family members to Indian City learned dance steps through observation and were strongly encouraged to enter the dance arena and dance whenever they could. Watching young dancers was a favorite for many visitors to Indian City.

ANADARKO INDIAN CITY USA

In one of the more recent postcard images from Indian City, a group of young Kiowa children stands in their regalia in front of a painted tipi. The two young girls wear traditional dresses made of wool broadcloth and decorated with cowrie shells. The young boy at right is wearing a buffalo headpiece and bone breastplate while he carries in his hands a fan and a dance stick.

Summer or winter, rain or shine, Indian City was open nearly every single day of the year. It functioned as a place of community for locals and a site of learning, exploration, and fun for the thousands of tourists who visited annually. In this image, two war dancers share their stories through dance against a colorful Oklahoma sunset during summertime.

Two

SHARING THROUGH DANCE, MUSIC, AND STORYTELLING

Young men and emerging dance champions demonstrated their dance moves to the beat of a hand drum. One of the biggest highlights of any visit to Indian City USA was being able to watch the dance and music shared, with some tourists even invited to participate in certain group social dances. Dancing and music involved most people employed at Indian City, whether or not they were official performers or guides.

The war dance was one of the most memorable and best-loved of the dance demonstrations, particularly given its fast pace and the bright colors of the regalia worn by the dancers. Traditionally only danced by men, this dance had its origins in the warrior societies to which many males belonged. These warrior societies were and still are the most important tribal organizations for men who have served in the military and returned to their communities as honored veterans. The war dance is meant to show the journey of a warrior on a war party. In the period before World War II, the war dance was set to a slower drum pace and the regalia worn by men was not as bold in color or flashy in decoration. After World War II, however, warriors dancing the war dance brought faster movements and quick footwork to the dance, as well as more brightly colored regalia.

Dixon Palmer (left) and Ernie Keahbone (center) drum and sing to accompany the war dance moves of George Palmer (right). Dancers in the post–World War II time wanted to show their individuality through their regalia and began to dress up their clothing with colorful bird feathers, including yellowhammer and cardinal feathers, and other adornments that were both natural and dyed. Wearing eagle feathers has long been considered a right that is earned and a badge of honor for dancers.

Young dancers demonstrate their war dance moves in front of the Wichita grass houses. These daily exhibitions of dance and music were timed so that they could perform for two groups simultaneously—with one visitor group beginning the tour and the other group finishing the tour. This schedule also meant that the location of the central dance ground was strategically located at the tour's starting place before visitors moved on to touring the traditional dwellings of tribal villages. The performances generally lasted for up to 20 minutes, often depending on the size, participation, and enthusiasm of the tourists watching.

Rudy Oheltoint (left) and Gus Palmer Jr. (right) demonstrate another all-male dance, the shield dance. Males adorned in colorful bustles would dance together with shields in hand. The movements of the dance were fast-paced and could represent a reenactment of a battle scene or could traditionally also serve as practice before battle.

A different pair of dancers demonstrates the shield dance while younger dancers look on from the arbor shade and get ready for their dances. Various shields with different patterns, including a turtle and hand prints, also hang from the arbor above.

Dixon Palmer poses with his hand-painted shield. The shields held by the dancers were notable for their painted patterns, with each shield bearing a unique image or pattern that was specific to the dancer, who had painted his own shield. Shields were often decorated based on a dancer's vision, dream, or memory of a battle scene.

A young dancer enters the dance arena with his colorful shield and a spear and is ready to begin the dance. This boy's shield is decorated with buffalo horns and eagle feathers.

Above, Paul Paddlety enters the dance arena with his painted shield and spear. An important part of male dance regalia for those dancers taking part in the war and shield dances was the feather bustles worn at the back. Below, young men are practicing their dance moves while wearing a variety of different feather bustles. Indian City USA was known within the community and across the region as a proving ground for up-and-coming dancers.

George Palmer (left) and Dixon Palmer (right) engage one another in a shield dance in front of the tipis at the Kiowa village. Nearly every single regalia item that was worn for dance, from head to toe, was handmade by George and Dixon.

Above, Truman Ware demonstrates the eagle dance in front of a tipi. Below, two dancers look on while another extends the eagle wings he wears. The eagle dance was another favorite of many visitors and again was primarily a male-only dance. For numerous tribal nations, the eagle has long been considered one of the most sacred animals on earth because of its unique ability to fly so high in the sky. This dance honored the eagle and its gift of flight, as well as being able to wear eagle feathers, as that was a privilege often earned by warriors. The male dancer is dressed as an eagle with a mask and a costume of feathers. In the Kiowa version of the eagle dance, the dancer's arms float with the beat of the drum, giving the impression of the dancer flying as the eagle does.

A young man demonstrates the hoop dance while the other sings. The hoop dance was regarded as a modern type of dance that arose in the 1920s and was often seen at Native events as a competition dance without any religious significance. The hoop dance was often performed at Indian City, with Dennis Begay remembered for being one of the best hoop dancers.

Tom Ware demonstrates the hoop dance as a young boy. While the hoop dance was performed primarily by men, females such as Georgette Palmer also danced and demonstrated fancy footwork. Hoops were normally made of willow branches, but nowadays many hoop dancers use plastic hoops.

To the left, George Oheltoint, a Kiowa war dancer and hoop dancer, demonstrates his skills with the hoops, as does another hoop dancer seen below wearing a roach. For performing the hoop dance, performers did not wear regalia that was as heavily adorned. This is because the focus of the hoop dance was for dancers to make different designs with the multiple hoops they handled, all the while dancing to a fast pace with the drum and demonstrating fancy footwork. Randy Palmer remembered that when he was hoop dancing, there were a lot of other young men who became interested and wanted to try it. He taught them some of his tricks, and they became hoop dancers who were able to perform for crowds.

Tom Ware was a talented flute player and dancer who spoke Comanche and Kiowa languages. He would often play flute for the tour groups that came through. Tom was also known as a great bead worker and a rock-and-roll musician. In the community, he was often called the "unofficial ambassador of Anadarko" because so many people knew him.

Harvey Keyonnie (left) performs a solo dance to the drumming done by Hugh Doyebi (right). Leonard Cozad was one of the main singers whose songs and drumming provided the music for dancers. Before working at Indian City, Cozad was a Kiowa code talker. His sons Lewis and Daniel also worked at Indian City and have been singing for all of their lives.

Above, dancer Harvey Keyonnie shows the feathered bustle he wears at the back, along with the bells he wears at his legs. In the image to the right, Keyonnie demonstrates dance steps in front of a tipi. The regalia worn by Keyonnie is noted for being the old style of war dance regalia since it included a cape that covered the shoulders.

Performances at Indian City would usually be concluded with social dances where tourists were invited to join, including the round dance, snake dance, and two-step. The round dance brought all participants together, holding hands and moving around a singer or drummer in a circular motion. The snake dance took the formation of a line following a leader. The two-step dance required couples to pair up and dance together, with a man and woman holding hands and coordinating their footsteps in time with the drum. The two-step dance is remembered as a favorite among many since it presented the opportunity for dancers to dance with someone they had a crush on.

Three

TRADITIONAL DWELLINGS OF NATIVE AMERICAN NATIONS

Lynda (left) and Randy Palmer (right) stand in front of an Apache wikiup dwelling while admiring a painted bison skull. At the center of each of the tribal villages were the traditional dwellings. These structures were reconstructed based on the knowledge and skills of tribal elders, along with the support and cooperation from the University of Oklahoma's Department of Anthropology.

This aerial photograph was taken in the late 1950s, not long after Indian City first opened. This image shows the initial structures on the Indian City property, including the lodge in the right upper corner. The earliest tribal dwellings to be erected at Indian City included the Kiowa tipis, Pawnee earth lodge, and Apache wikiups, with the Wichita and Caddo dwellings following behind not long after. In this image, the largest of the Wichita grass houses is still under construction.

Oklahoma Indian Grass House

Several Wichita grass houses dotted the Indian City property. These beehive-shaped grass houses were the traditional dwellings of the Wichita Tribe, one of the tribes to call Oklahoma its original homeland. As seen in both images, the largest of the grass houses, called the "Council house," was estimated by Randy Palmer to stand about 10 feet higher than a telephone pole. This height allowed the grass house to be a place where young employees of Indian City could gather to play badminton and volleyball inside when tourists were not around. During the winter months, the dancers and employees often built a fire inside and came together to dance. Inside these grass houses, the Wichita people traditionally used corncobs and feathers to make little birds that functioned like a mobile above the fireplace. These served to catch upward drafts so that the smoke from the fire could exit straight above through the roof hole.

Leather bands were used to fasten the bundles of spinifex grass together. It was important that those bands were covered so that the leather would not rot when the rain came and water ran off the sides. Using these different materials, the bundled grass could function almost like shingles on a roof and a rain gutter that helped to funnel the water away. Randy recalls that he and many of the other men working at Indian City were taught grass house construction by Mac Stevenson.

While the Caddo Tribe was also known to construct grass house dwellings, the Caddo homes at Indian City were built in the manner of wooden cabins with upright poles and wattle-and-daub roofs. The roof of the cabin was made with wooden poles. A lattice of willows was tied to these supports, and grass was attached and secured to the lattice. During the colder months, a fire could also be built inside the structures. An opening in the center of the roof allowed the smoke of the fire to travel out. The original homelands of the Caddo people spanned parts of Louisiana, eastern Texas, Arkansas, and southeastern Oklahoma. These wooden cabins suited the warmer climate the Caddos experienced in their homeland area.

The Pawnee earth lodge was built with its base firmly submerged in the ground. The circular frame of the lodge was constructed with eight wooden poles that were expertly layered and covered with soil. In addition to serving as home dwellings and places for gathering, these earth lodge structures also were built to function as astronomical observatories, allowing Pawnee people to observe the movement of stars in the night sky. Traditional Pawnee astronomical knowledge has always held a place of extreme significance for tribal members. Randy Palmer also remembers that inside the earth lodge at Indian City was a traditional calendar printed on a bison hide that marked important events during specific seasons.

As seen above, the entrance to the Pawnee earth lodge could look slightly different according to the seasons, which would change the color of the grass growing across the structure. Below, next to the stretched bison hide, stands a sign that offers information on Pawnee people and culture. The homelands of the Pawnee people are in Nebraska, but the tribe was forcibly removed to Indian Territory in the 1870s. Unlike many of the other tribes at Indian City, the Pawnee tribal headquarters are not near Anadarko but are based in north-central Oklahoma in the town of Pawnee. The Pawnee people have long maintained strong ties to the Wichita Tribe, and the languages of the Pawnee, Caddo, and Wichita peoples are closely related.

There were numerous Kiowa tipis at Indian City. The tipi was by far the most recognizable traditional Native American dwelling for tourists. At Indian City, visitors would learn about the diversity of tipis and how painted decorations on tipis reflected specific family designs and cultural symbols. Importantly, tourists also were informed of the fact that tipis were not the only traditional Native American dwelling of the southern plains, helping to debunk a common stereotype.

Indian City USA...

The only authentic restoration of American dwellings and way of life in America, Indian City U.S.A. is on the site of the massacre of the Tonkawa Indians by a band of Shawnees and other mercenaries during the Civil War.

Truly authentic in every detail, the villages of Indian City U.S.A. were planned by and constructed under the supervision of the Department of Anthropology, University of Oklahoma.

A living memorial to the American Indian, a tour of the villages of Indian city U.S.A. is a treat for everyone interested in Indian life.

There are four Annual Indian Ceremonials held at Indian City U.S.A. each year; call or write for information.

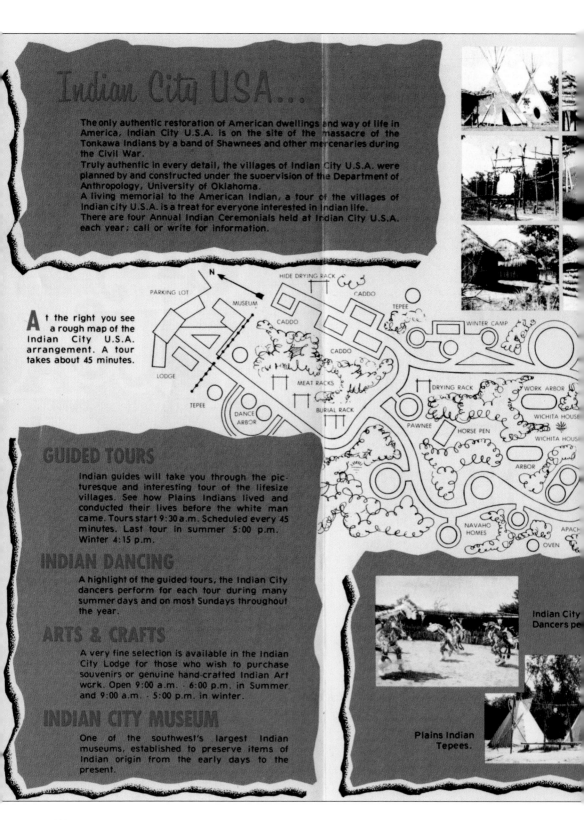

At the right you see a rough map of the Indian City U.S.A. arrangement. A tour takes about 45 minutes.

GUIDED TOURS

Indian guides will take you through the picturesque and interesting tour of the lifesize villages. See how Plains Indians lived and conducted their lives before the white man came. Tours start 9:30 a.m. Scheduled every 45 minutes. Last tour in summer 5:00 p.m. Winter 4:15 p.m.

INDIAN DANCING

A highlight of the guided tours, the Indian City dancers perform for each tour during many summer days and on most Sundays throughout the year.

ARTS & CRAFTS

A very fine selection is available in the Indian City Lodge for those who wish to purchase souvenirs or genuine hand-crafted Indian Art work. Open 9:00 a.m. - 6:00 p.m. in Summer and 9:00 a.m. - 5:00 p.m. in winter.

INDIAN CITY MUSEUM

One of the southwest's largest Indian museums, established to preserve items of Indian origin from the early days to the present.

Indian City Dancers pe

Plains Indian Tepees.

Original Anadarko Indian Agency built in 1880.

Other Places To See and Visit

- SOUTHERN PLAINS INDIAN MUSEUM AND CRAFTS CENTER   Anadarko, Highway 62 East
- THE NATIONAL HALL OF FAME FOR FAMOUS AMERICAN INDIANS, Anadarko, Highway 62 East
- PHILOMATHIC PIONEER MUSEUM, Anadarko Rock Island Depot
- RIVERSIDE INDIAN SCHOOL, north of Anadarko
- RED ROCK CANYON STATE PARK, Hinton, 40 minutes north
- WICHITA MOUNTAINS WILDLIFE REFUGE, Lawton, 1 hour south
- FORT SILL ARTILLERY & MISSLE CENTER Lawton, 45 minutes south
- MUSEUM OF THE GREAT PLAINS, Lawton, 1 hour south
- FORT COBB RESERVOIR STATE PARK, 25 minutes northwest
- QUARTZ MOUNTAIN STATE LODGE, Altus, 1½ hours southwest

Thunderbird Campground

RESERVATIONS 405/247-5661 or 1-800-433-5661

A camper's view of the campground of Indian City. Sites range from full service to a spot under the trees nestled in a valley of the old Indian country. Swimming pool and picnic grounds available.

This map of Indian City from the 1970s shows the layout of the villages and some of the other highlights along the tour trail, including specific arbors for dance, work, and rest, as well as racks for drying meat. The inclusion of other tribal dwellings shows that the tribal villages grew and expanded since the first days of Indian City's opening. Additional information provided on the right panel of the map informed tourists about the campground accommodations for those wanting to camp, as well as other cultural and natural attractions in southwest Oklahoma.

Above, the Kiowa winter camp is pictured on a bright, sunny day. Kiowa tipis normally face east toward the direction of the rising sun. Kiowa homelands encompassed much of the eastern side of the Rocky Mountains, with Kiowa migrations in later centuries leading them down into the southern plains of Oklahoma. Under the 1867 Treaty of Medicine Lodge, the Kiowa Tribe was assigned a reservation in Oklahoma in 1868. In the image below, two Indian City guides speak to one another in front of four canvas tipis, showing the scale of how tall tipis and tipi poles were in relation to people.

Indian City dancers speak to one another in front of a painted tipi depicting a battle scene. The Palmer family was well known for the tipis that they made and decorated with painted designs. Randy's mother, Chlotiea Palmer, was able to sew the canvas of one whole tipi together in about a day and a half. Randy's father, Dixon, was the one to paint the tipis. In the early days of Indian City, Delores and Homer Buffalo were also noted tipi makers. Delores would construct and sew the canvas covers, while Homer would erect the poles and raise the tipis. In the 1960s, this couple was noted to have built one of the last buffalo-hide tipis in Oklahoma. That tipi required about 15 buffalo skins, and Delores recalled that it took a full month to make by hand-sewing it with buffalo sinew as the thread.

In the image above, Kiowa-Apache tour guide Elton Stumbling Bear stands in front of a traditional Apache wikiup. Apache wikiups were constructed with the use of wooden poles, often from the willow tree but also from whatever was available to construct a frame. These poles were driven into the ground and then covered with brush and grass. These dome-shaped structures were smaller than the Wichita grass houses. When Apaches moved to a new campsite, they would take their hides and possessions, leaving the frame behind, since a new one could easily be constructed. The ease of constructing this wikiup dwelling facilitated the traditionally nomadic lifestyle of Apache people. Randy recalls that of all the traditional dwellings at Indian City, the wikiups were the quickest to assemble and set up.

During the wintertime or rain, Apache wikiups could be covered by animal hides to provide extra insulation and warmth to those who dwelled inside of the structure. Apache homelands have traditionally encompassed desert, canyon, mountain, and southern plains landscapes throughout the southwestern and southern United States. There are nine different federally recognized Apache tribes in the United States, with the majority located in Arizona and New Mexico. Oklahoma is home to two of these Apache tribes, the Apache Tribe of Oklahoma and the Fort Sill Apache Tribe of Oklahoma. Members of the Apache Tribe of Oklahoma are also often referred to as "Kiowa-Apache" or "Plains Apache," given their close historical ties with the Kiowas.

The hogan is the traditional dwelling of the Navajo people, who call themselves Diné people, and one stood at Indian City. In addition to the Navajo hogan, there was also a Pueblo adobe structure. Navajo and Pueblo tribes have firm roots in the southwestern United States, with 19 sovereign Pueblo nations throughout New Mexico and the Navajo Nation covering the four corners region of New Mexico, Arizona, and Utah. Neither the Navajo nor the Pueblo tribes were based in Oklahoma, but their inclusion at Indian City was based on the fact that tourists were interested in the cultures of these well-known tribes. The Pueblo adobe structure was the very last of the traditional dwellings to be built.

Four

EVERYDAY LIFEWAYS AND CULTURAL ACTIVITIES

Dixon Palmer is wearing his full dance regalia and demonstrates how to shoot an arrow. Behind him is a tipi that he had painted on the site of the original Kiowa village. As Indian City grew and expanded, the Kiowa camp was relocated elsewhere on the grounds, and in its place, a Pueblo adobe structure was built to show an example of a traditional Pueblo dwelling.

Hugh Doyebi stands in full dance regalia and displays a pipe. Pipes are important items that have long been used ceremonially, since tobacco was integral to prayers and spiritual offerings. The sharing of a pipe formed important bonds between men. When used ceremonially, the smoke from the pipe is understood as going up to the Creator as an offering.

An elder sits outside of the Wichita grass house putting finishing touches on a cradleboard for a newborn. Cradleboards were and continue to be used among numerous tribal communities as a way of keeping a baby safe and snug. Many cradleboards could be tied onto a mother's back so that she could easily transport her baby while traveling. Cradleboards were also often decorated with designs and patterns that were specific to the tribe or the family. To the left of this lady are drying cobs of corn and squash, important staples of the diets of agrarian plains tribes such as the Wichitas and Caddos, among others.

Dixon Palmer (left) points while holding on to a travois. The travois was a wooden structure commonly used by different tribes as a sledge to help transport items when people were moving. Normally consisting of two long wooden poles fastened together with smaller poles that would support the load, the travois was first pulled by dogs. Later, with the spread of horse culture among plains tribes, the travois was hooked onto horses.

Kiowa guide Winston Cat Oyebi stands next to a travois. Winston wears a ribbon shirt, which is commonly worn among different Native American men and is a piece of clothing that has become pan-tribal. On the poles behind Winston are pieces of cloth painted to look like meat jerky that has been sliced and is drying in the sun. Meat jerky, particularly bison jerky, has long been a traditional staple food of Kiowas and other plains tribes.

Dancer and guide Paul Paddlety stands next to the stretched bison hide in the Kiowa winter camp part of the village. He explains how the hides were scraped to make buckskin that was used for tipis and clothing while the fur was kept as stuffing for pillows.

Two women working at Indian City carefully cut and trim all pieces of meat from a cow carcass. These strips of meat are hung on the poles behind them and sun-dried to make beef jerky, a local favorite and traditional food among those living and working at Indian City.

THELMA TOEHAY

NATHAN WOLFE

MADELEINE TORRES

MARY FRANCES KEYE

LENORA BOYIDDLE

VINCENT PALMER

LA RONDA ROULAIN

*Cover: PAINTED VA
1972, made by Thelma T
hay, Kiowa-Apache
painted by William Ton(
hote, Kiowa. (72.34.1)*

"I enjoy making pottery. I learned how to make pottery in one week. I would rather make potter
han design (paint) because when you make pottery you have different shapes to make and you neve
et bored..."

Thelma Toeha

"I like it. It's a job where a person can express himself in the designs that he puts on the pots..."

Nathan Wolf(

"I like this work. I'm just starting to catch on but I enjoy it. I also beadwork but I like this bet
er..."

Madeleine Torre:

"I really like this work and enjoy doing it..."

Mary Frances Keye:

"I like working here at the Indian City Pottery plant. I like what I'm doing..."

Lenora Boyiddl(

"This work is okay..."

Vincent Palme:

"I enjoy pottery work and in a way it's challenging..."

LaRonda Roulai:

This brochure features information on Indian City pottery from a 1974 exhibition focused on the
pottery that was held by the neighboring Southern Plains Indian Museum in Anadarko. Because
pottery was an item in such high demand at the shop in the lodge, the Indian City Pottery initiative
was begun to provide a consistent supply for eager tourists ready to buy these unique pieces. The
original initiative also involved instruction and training of a group of 15 apprentices, including
Kiowa-Apache artist Thelma Toehay, who was also noted as an accomplished bead worker. After

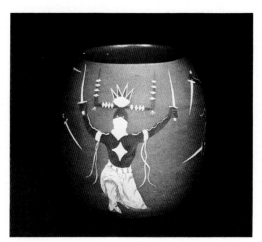

PAINTED VASE, 1973, made by Thelma Toehay, Kiowa-Apache and painted by Dorothy Palmer, Kiowa-Choctaw. (73.15.1)

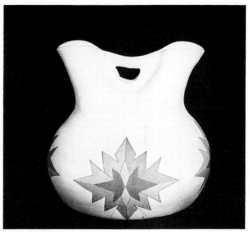

PAINTED WEDDING JAR, 1973, made by Thelma Toehay, Kiowa-Apache and painted by Dixon Palmer, Kiowa-Choctaw.

RELIGIOUS UTENSILS, 1972, made by Thelma Toehay, Kiowa-Apache and painted by Dixon Palmer, Kiowa-Choctaw. (72.14.4)

PAINTED VASE, 1973, made by Thelma Toehay, Kiowa-Apache and painted by William Tonepahote, Kiowa. (73.10)

using a potter's wheel to shape the pieces, the pots were dried for several days before being sanded and glazed. Pottery would then be painted, and designs ranged from geometric shapes to realistic and representational images. The final step for the pottery involved eight hours of firing in an electric kiln before it was ready to be sold. (Courtesy Southern Plains Indian Museum and Crafts Center.)

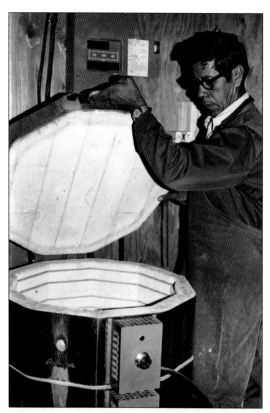

Dixon Palmer lifts the kiln lid to check on the progress of the pottery during the firing process. For a number of years, Dixon was manager of the Indian City Pottery business and helped to increase production and encouraged the development of new designs.

Members of the Palmer family, including Dixon and Vincent (left side), are busy painting the dried pots with intricate designs in the Indian City Pottery studio.

Above, Hugh Doyebi stands in front of a painted buffalo skull showing the intricacy of the dance regalia that he wears. Below, the Palmer family dancers present the movements of the war dance. Dorothy Whitehorse Delaune remembered that what helped make Indian City such a great place for so many Native youth was that people such as Dixon Palmer and others "were instructing as they were going along and performing for tourists."

INDIAN CITY, U.S.A. - OKLAHOMA

The younger generations at Indian City continue to share their cultural stories and traditions. With the newer generations of dancers at Indian City came new styles not only in dance movements but also in regalia. Both of these young men can be seen to wear a more contemporary style of feathered bustles at the back that allow them to give additional flair during their fancy dance movements.

Above is a funeral site with two elevated scaffolds. Traditionally, the bodies of the deceased would be wrapped in buffalo hides. The possessions of the deceased, such as bows and arrows or a horse, were tied to the poles so that those possessions could accompany the deceased. Eventually, the body returns to the earth. While this was the practice of some of the plains tribes, such as the Kiowa, this was not the protocol followed by other agrarian tribes, such as the Caddo or Wichita peoples.

On the board sign in front is written, "In Memory of Hunting Horse, Kiowa." This memorial was for Old Man "Tsa-Toke" Hunting Horse, who was an esteemed member of the Kiowa Tribe and had served as a scout for the US Army. Tsa-Toke lived from 1846 to 1953 and had 10 children, including Monroe Tsatoke, one of the Kiowa Five artists.

Kiowa-Apache Clessa Little Chief and her daughters Glenda (left) and Kathy (right) stand in front of a painted tipi in the Kiowa village. All three of the ladies wear cloth dresses that were appropriate for the sweltering summer months in Oklahoma. When among themselves in between tours and during the quieter months, Randy Palmer recalls that most people working at Indian City would sit under the arbors or within traditional dwellings and talk about traditional lifeways, as well as share funny stories and memories.

Five

NOTABLE FAMILIES OF INDIAN CITY AND THE LEGACY OF KIOWA WARRIOR SOCIETIES

Beyond serving as a treasured tourism attraction and site of cultural education over decades, the land upon which Indian City sits has held other extremely important purposes for Kiowa tribal members. Indian City has long been the place where Kiowa veterans have come to gather for yearly dances as key activities of the Kiowa warrior societies, in particular the Kiowa Black Leggings Warrior Society and Oh Ho Ma Society. In this image, Kiowa Black Leggings members and war veterans line up to enter the central tipi to be cedared and blessed. (Courtesy Lester Harragarra.)

One of the most esteemed and knowledgeable Kiowa elders to have worked at Indian City was Frank Bosin, along with his family. Bosin worked at Indian City from its initial opening and shared his knowledge with other Indian City employees and visitors over the years. In this image, Bosin is cloaked in a bison skin and stands in front of the Pawnee earth lodge.

Above, Nathan Doyebi (left), his wife Ruby Doyebi (center), and Dixon Palmer sing and drum together as part of a program for visitors in front of the Wichita village. Nathan was one of the very first drummers to perform regularly at Indian City from the day that it opened. During the wintertime, when crowds were slightly smaller, the Doyebis were known to make pieces of art and crafts that were often sold in the lodge. Nathan was known for his skills in painting and woodwork. To the right, Nathan Doyebi provides the drumming and singing for dancers at Indian City.

Leonard Cozad, Sr.

Above, Leonard Cozad Sr. was known throughout Indian Country and across the United States for his gifts of singing and drumming. He and his family were involved with Indian City from early on. Leonard Cozad Sr. was a prolific composer of Kiowa songs, and many of the songs still sung around the drum today are his compositions. This profound musical legacy has continued through many of his children and relatives to this day. Below, Leonard Sr. is seated second from the left around the drum along with two of his sons and other drummers. (Both, courtesy Rudy Bantista, Kiowa Black Leggings Warrior Society.)

Left to right: Rusty Cozad, Leonard Cozad, Sr., Leonard Cozad, Jr., Woodcoy Santos and Jack Anquoe.

From left to right, Clara Auchita, Anna Sue Whitehorse, Lynda Palmer, and Beauty Bosin gather together in front of the Indian City entrance on a sunny day. They are sitting together and working on beadwork projects that will be sold in the lodge for tourists eager to purchase authentic and handmade Native art and crafts.

Seen here from left to right, Ruby Turkey Doyebi, Chlotiea Palmer, Beauty Bosin, and Anna Sue Nimsey are gathered together indoors working on beading projects when the weather was colder.

George Palmer (left) and his wife, Imogene (center), both extremely active at Indian City over decades, stand and speak with dignitaries in London, England. During this trip in March 1971, the Palmers gave a British museum a full war dancer regalia set, and the Palmers were also able to have an audience with Queen Elizabeth II. Imogene had done the beadwork and George completed the featherwork on the dance regalia.

Dixon Palmer Sr. (center) stands with his son Randy (right) inside of the Pawnee earth lodge, where he tells visitors about the dwelling and the traditional calendar painted on the bison hide behind them. The Palmers were one of the most active families at Indian City, with Dixon serving as a key dancer, storyteller, regalia maker, painter, and knowledge holder. In this image, Randy is listening and learning from his father how to share information on a tour.

From left to right, Mark Keahbone, George Palmer, Dixon Palmer, and Puppy Littlejoe stand in front of a tipi in 1959 or 1960 in one of the early years of the revival of the Kiowa Black Leggings Society. Men's warrior societies had always been one of the most important elements of traditional Kiowa life that centered on the tribe's respect for veterans and the warrior tradition. Revived by returning veterans from World Wars I and II in 1958, these veterans sought the guidance of their elders to bring life back to these traditions. (Courtesy Rudy Bantista, Kiowa Black Leggings Warrior Society.)

Above, Black Leggings members proudly enter the dance arena. The Black Leggings Warrior Society is known in Kiowa as "Ton-Kon-Ga," and it follows traditional protocols related to songs, dances, ceremonies, and the dress code of its members, particularly during its annual dance ceremony. The Black Leggings Society has always been a male-only society, but women are actively involved in the dances, ceremonies, and preparation to honor and celebrate their male kinfolk who are veterans, as seen below. The ceremonies and dances of Black Leggings comprise Kiowa veterans and their participating families. Visitors are welcome to observe the ceremony.

Dixon Palmer Sr. dances during the Black Leggings Warrior Society dance. Dixon was a World War II US Army veteran who had served 511 days in combat in Europe as a member of the 45th Division. While in the Army and stationed in Massachusetts, Dixon formed a dance group that presented performances all over the US East Coast. Dixon worked for decades at Indian City after his Army career and continued as a master dancer and regalia maker. Thanks to the close relationship between the Palmers and the Moran family who managed Indian City, the grounds below Indian City were designated as a place for Kiowa warrior societies to gather, including the Black Leggings and Oh Ho Ma Societies.

Pictured above, at the beginning of the ceremony, the veterans of the Black Leggings Society line up to enter the central tipi, where they are blessed and prayed over with cedar smoke. This battle tipi sits within the dance grounds and was painted by Sherman Chaddlesone. After the members are blessed, they exit the tipi and line up in anticipation of the initial dance when the veterans enter the arena, as seen below. (Both, courtesy Lester Harragarra.)

Throughout this ceremony, individual men can have particular songs that are sung during the dance, and specific veterans can be honored for particular deeds or accomplishments. Male veteran members wear a red cape to honor the past Ton-Kon-Ga chief Gool-Hay-Ee, who had killed a Mexican officer during a battle and wore his red cape as a trophy of the battle. (Courtesy Lester Harragarra.)

Female relatives of Black Leggings Warrior Society members line up next to the battle tipi to dance and honor their male kinfolk, whether the veterans are their husbands, sons, grandsons, fathers, or grandfathers. Within the Black Leggings Society, there are four members—two boys and two girls—who serve a special role. The Ah-Day-Mahton, or "Favorite Girl," and Ah-Day-Tal-Lee, or "Favorite Boy," are raised from a young age within the Black Leggings Society and taught traditional Kiowa duties, protocols, and behaviors until the age of 17 or 18, when they step down and hand the role to others. (Courtesy Lester Harragarra.)

To this day, the Indian City grounds serve as a well-loved gathering place for the Kiowa Black Leggings Warrior Society and Oh Ho Ma Society. New members are brought in nearly every year to these warrior societies as Kiowa veterans proudly return from their military service. (Courtesy Lester Harragarra.)

Randy and Lynda Palmer stand center in front of a hide tipi in the Indian City Kiowa camp, with Anna Sue Whitehorse (right) and other ladies proudly displaying the US flag. Indian City is a place where traditional culture is shared, numerous Native veterans were proudly employed, and Kiowa warrior societies including Black Leggings and Oh Ho Ma are a legacy that continues strong into the present.

Six

AN IMPORTANT FACE
OF OKLAHOMA
TO THE WORLD

Even in postcards that promoted Oklahoma or Indian Country more generally, images of Indian City can be found. Over its nearly 55-year history, Indian City welcomed tens of thousands of people from across the country and the globe. Dorothy Whitehorse Delaune recalls that there were often chartered buses coming with visitors from Japan and across Europe, and overflow parking was required at the bottom of the hill. A tractor served as the shuttle for getting larger groups up to the lodge on the hill.

ROUTE U.S. 66

OKLA

LITTLE "NONNIE"

YUKON

WEATHERFORD   EL RENO   40

TEXOLA 66   40   66

↓ ERICK   CLINTON   CHICKASHA

ELK CITY   TO ANADARKO
            "INDIAN CITY U.S.A"
SAYRE   TO WICHITA FALLS & FORT WORTH

NATIONAL COWBOY HALL OF FAME   OKLAHOMA

Oklahoma is the literal heart of the famed Route 66 cross-country highway, and the state is known for being home to the longest stretch of drivable Route 66 road miles. Traveling along Route 66, visitors to Indian City would only need to exit south at Highway 281 heading toward Hinton,

Binger, and Gracemont to then reach Anadarko. Thus, the legacies of Route 66 and Indian City are closely intertwined. In 2026, Route 66 is planning to celebrate its centennial anniversary throughout Oklahoma.

Dixon Palmer Sr. stands on a ladder and paints a welcoming mural of traditional images on the edge of the cliff face that comprises one side of Indian City. This spirit of community, tradition, learning, and welcome is one that continues to characterize the memories of those who worked and lived at Indian City over decades.

From left to right, Tim Nestell, Bobbie Chew Bigby, Randy Palmer, Donna Jean Tsatoke, and Lois Tsatoke stand together on Memorial Day weekend in 2023 to share and record stories about Indian City USA at the Palmer family home. This project has been centered in community memories and propelled forward by a desire to keep younger generations invested in and passionate about their traditional cultures and connections to the community.

Dixon Palmer Sr. (center) dances at a Black Leggings Warrior Society ceremony in the late 1990s. Throughout the process of storytelling, recording, and researching for this book, Bobbie Chew Bigby and the Palmer family have been continuously reminded of the importance of veterans to their lives, families, and this country. Part of the proceeds from the sale of this book will be donated to the Wounded Warrior Project.

BIBLIOGRAPHY

Bantista, R. *Kiowa Black Leggings Warrior Society 25th Anniversary*. Indian City, OK: Kiowa Black Leggings Society, 1983.

Boulton, J.R. "Delores Buffalo Takes Us to Indian City." *Oklahoma Today* 30, no. 2 (1980): 16–18.

Clark, B. *Indian Tribes of Oklahoma*. Norman: University of Oklahoma Press, 2020.

Connole, J. "A Terrible Truth: The Tonkawa Massacre of 1862." *The Chronicles of Oklahoma* 97, no. 4 (Winter 2019).

Corntassel, J., T. Alfred, N. Goodyear-Kaṡōpua, N.K. Silva, H.K. Aikau, and D. Mucina. *Everyday Acts of Resurgence: People, Places, Practices*. Olympia, WA: Daykeeper Press, 2018.

Hatfield, L. "Indian City U.S.A." *Oklahoma Today* 6, no. 5 (1956): 10–11.

Hedglen, T.L. "American Indian Exposition." *The Encyclopedia of Oklahoma History and Culture*. January 15, 2010. www.okhistory.org/publications/enc/entry?entry=AM005.

May, J.D. "Tonkawa Massacre." *The Encyclopedia of Oklahoma History and Culture*. January 15, 2010. www.okhistory.org/publications/enc/entry?entry=TO005.

Stokely, M. "Picturing the People: Kiowa, Comanche, and Plains Apache Postcards." *Plains Anthropologist* 60 no. 234 (2015): 99–123.

Wright, M.H. "The American Indian Exposition in Oklahoma." *The Chronicles of Oklahoma* 24 (1946): 158–165.

DISCOVER THOUSANDS OF LOCAL HISTORY BOOKS FEATURING MILLIONS OF VINTAGE IMAGES

Arcadia Publishing, the leading local history publisher in the United States, is committed to making history accessible and meaningful through publishing books that celebrate and preserve the heritage of America's people and places.

Find more books like this at
www.arcadiapublishing.com

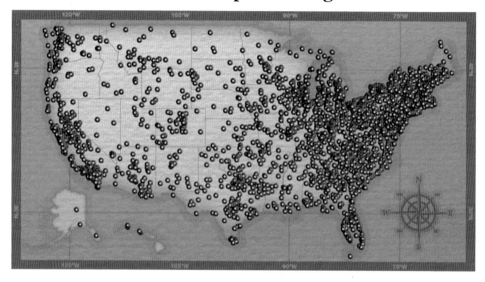

Search for your hometown history, your old stomping grounds, and even your favorite sports team.